P9-DFX-415

Ashley

Ashley
Gambler

AMERICA'S
NATURAL BEAUTY

A nobler want of man
is served by nature,
namely, the love of beauty. . . .
Nature is loved
by what is best in us.
It is loved
as the city of God

Ralph Waldo Emerson

Ideals Publishing Corporation
Nashville, Tennessee

PHOTOS

6-7: Color photos courtesy of Acadia National Park, black and whites from Library of Congress; 8-9: Jeff Gnass Photography; 10-11: Photos courtesy of the New Hampshire Department of Parks and Recreation; 12-13: Dick Dietrich Photography; 14: Archive Photos/Peter Lucas; 15: Archive Photos; 16-17: William Johnson/Johnson's Photography; 18-19: Library of Congress; 20-21: William Johnson/Johnson's Photography; 22-23: Library of Congress; 24-25: Dick Dietrich Photography; 26: Photos courtesy of Pictured Rocks National Lakeshore and the National Park Service; 27: Photos courtesy of Alger County Historical Society and Pictured Rocks National Lakeshore; 28-29: Jess Gnass Photography; 32-33: Photos courtesy of Assateague Island National Seashore; 34-35: D. Muench/H. Armstrong Roberts; 36: Photo courtesy of the National Park Service-37: Color photo courtesy of the National Park Service, black and white from the Library of Congress; 38-39: G. Ahrens/H. Armstrong Roberts; 40-41: Photos courtesy of Cape Hatteras National Seashore; 42-43: William Johnson/Johnson's Photography; 44-45: Photos courtesy of Great Smoky Mountains National Park; 46-47: Dick Dietrich Photography; 48: Archive Photos/Max Hunn, Library of Congress; 49: Laatsch-Hupp Photo/ Lois E. Clarke; 50-51: W. Bertsch/H. Armstrong Roberts; 56-57: William Johnson/Johnson's Photography; 58-59: Photos courtesy of Guadalupe Mountains National Park; 60-61: Jeff Gnass Photography; 62-63: Photos courtesy of Carlsbad Caverns National Park/National Park Service; 64-65: H. Armstrong Roberts; 66: Archive Photos/Frank E. Gunnel; 67: Archive Photos/Hirz; 68-69: Jeff Gnass Photography; 70-71: Photos courtesy of Petrified Forest National Park/National Park Service; 72-73: Dick Dietrich Photography; 74-75: Photos courtesy of Grand Canyon National Park/National Park Service; 76-77: Dick Dietrich Photography; 78-79: Photos courtesy of Sequoia and King's Canyon National Park; 80-81: Dick Dietrich Photography; 82-83: Photos courtesy of Channel Islands National Park/National Park Service; 84-85: Jeff Gnass Photography; 86-87: Library of Congress; 88-89: Jeff Gnass Photography; 91: Library of Congress; 92-93: D. Muench/H. Armstrong Roberts; 94-95: Photos courtesy of Bryce Canyon National Park; 96-97: Jeff Gnass Photography; 98-99: Photos courtesy of Arches National Park; 100-101:Dick Dietrich Photography; 102-103: Library of Congress; 104-105: Dick Dietrich Photography; 108-109: Photos courtesy of Crater Lake National Park; 110-111: Jeff Gnass Photography; 114-115: Jeff Gnass Photography; 116: Photos courtesy of Glacier National Park; 118-119: Dick Dietrich Photography; 120-121: Photos courtesy of Yellowstone National Park; 122-123: Jeff Gnass Photography; 124-125: Photos courtesy of Yellowstone National Park; 126-127: Jeff Gnass Photography; 128-129: Photos courtesy of Grand Teton National Park; 130-131: Jeff Gnass Photography; 132-133: Color photos courtesy of Badlands National Park, black and white from Archive Photos/Frank Gunnel; 134-135: Jeff Gnass Photography; 138-139: Photos courtesy of Kenai Fjords National Park; 140-141: Jeff Gnass Photography; 142-143: Photos courtesy of Denali National Park/National Park Service; 144-145: Jeff Gnass Photography; 146-147: Photo courtesy Kenai Fjords National Park; 148-149: Jeff Gnass Photography; 150-151: Photos courtesy of Haleakala National Park; 152-153: Jeff Gnass Photography; 154-155: Photos courtesy J. D. Griggs/U.S. Geological Survey; 156-157: Jeff Gnass Photography

ACKNOWLEDGMENTS

Our sincere thanks to Marjory Stoneman Douglas, whom we were unable to contact.
Illustrations by SusanHarrison and Tim Peterson.
Book design by Patrick McRae.

Copyright © 1992 by Ideals Publishing Corporation
All rights reserved. No part of this publication may be reproduced
or transmitted in any form or by any means, electronic or mechancal,
including photocopy, recording, or any information storage and retrieval
system, without permission in writing from the publisher.

Published by Ideals Publishing Corporation
565 Marriott Drive
Nashville, Tennessee 37214

Printed and bound in the United States of America.

ISBN 0-8249-4048-2

The text type was set in Caslon 540.
The display type was set in Caslon Swash
Color separations were made by Web Tech of Milwaukee, Wisconsin.
Printed and bound by Ringier America, New Berlin, Wisconsin.

Cover Photo: The Grand Canyon, Arizona, Dick Dietrich Photography

CONTENTS

THE BEAUTY
OF THE
NORTHEAST

4

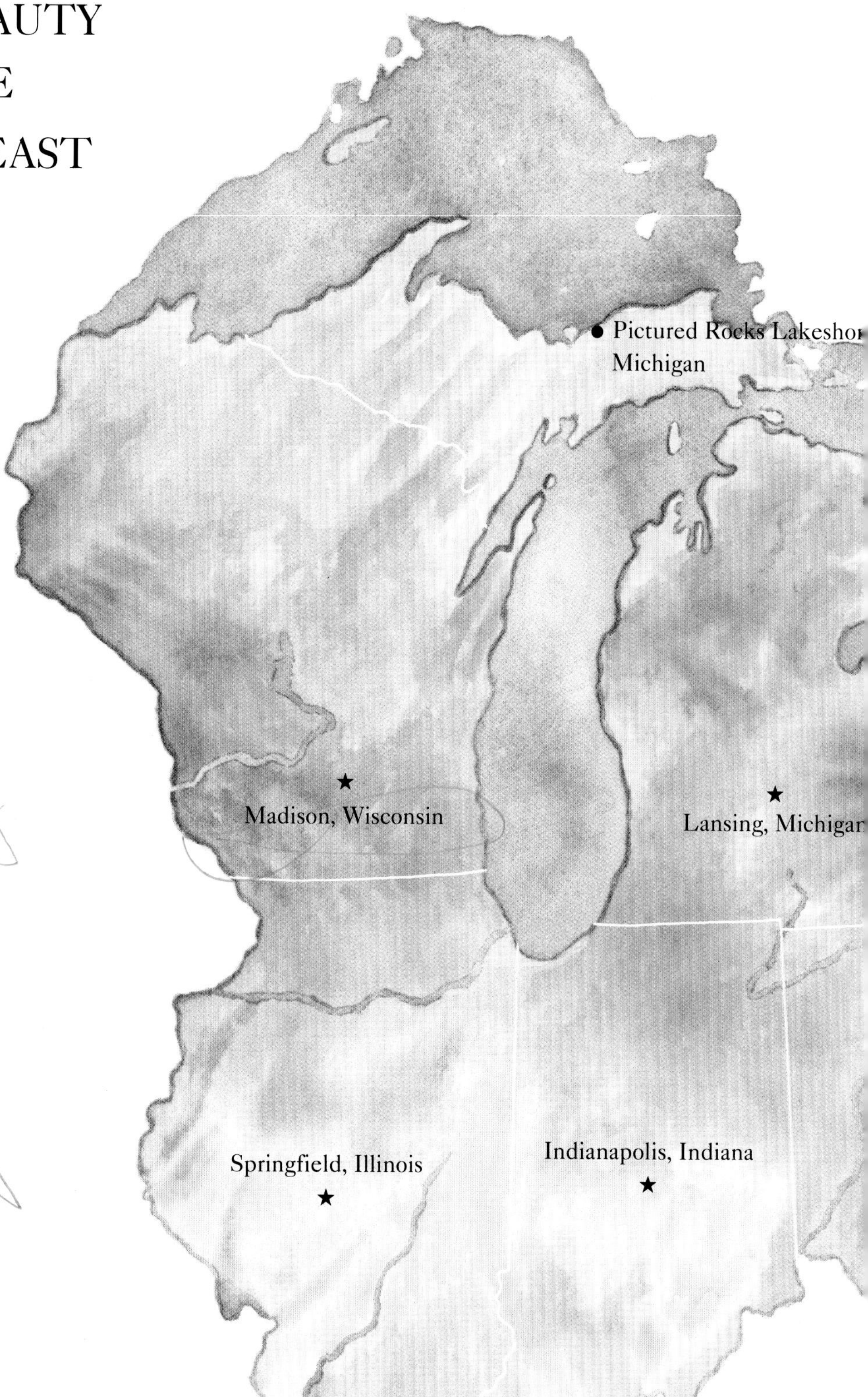

● Pictured Rocks Lakeshore
Michigan

★
Madison, Wisconsin

★
Lansing, Michigan

Springfield, Illinois
★

Indianapolis, Indiana
★

*The scenes of the Northeast are
comfortable and familiar—the cold spray
of the Atlantic on a rocky beach,
the broad, sloping peaks of
a time-worn mountain, the vibrant colors of
October reflected on a still, blue lake.*

Augusta, Maine ★

Montpelier, Vermont ★

● Franconia Notch,
New Hampshire

Adirondack Mountains, ●
New York

★ Concord, New Hampshire

Albany, New York ★

★ Boston, Massachusetts

Cape Cod, Massachusetts ●

● Niagara Falls, New York

★ Providence,
Rhode Island

★ Hartford, Connecticut

Harrisburg, Pennsylvania ★

★ Trenton, New Jersey

Columbus, Ohio

★ Dover,
Delaware

Mt. Desert Island lies off the northern coast of Maine. The island's diverse terrain includes rocky cliffs, dense forests, and broad, sloping mountains.

Cornus canadensis
- Bunchberry -

6

Rising 1,530 feet above sea level on the eastern shore of the island is Cadillac Mountain, the highest point along the Atlantic coast.

Rocky cliffs along the shores of Mt. Desert Island

Thunder Hole, named for the sound of the crashing surf

Located in the center of Mt. Desert Island is Somes Sound, the only true fjord in the lower forty-eight states. A fjord is a narrow inlet in the sea surrounded by cliffs or steep slopes.

The island owes its name to French explorer Samuel de Champlain, who discovered the land in 1604 while mapping the shores of New France. He called his discovery *L'isle des Monts-déserts,* or "the island of barren mountains."

Sailboats fill the waters off Bar Harbor

Larus argentatus
-Herring Gull-

More than 275 species of birds inhabit Mt. Desert Island; 500 varieties of wildflowers add their color to the island from late April through mid-summer.

acer saccharum
-Sugar Maple-

7

In fall, the slopes of Mt. Desert Island's mountains flame with color. The display is more intense since the Great Fire of October 1947, which destroyed 17,000 acres of evergreen forest and made room for the changeable foliage of aspen, birch, and maple trees.

The Louisburg Hotel, Bar Harbor, 1901

Littorina obtusata
-Northern Yellow Periwinkle-

Most of Mt. Desert Island is included in Acadia National Park, the only national park in New England, the oldest park east of the Mississippi, and the first park donated to the government by private landowners for use by the American public.

Eagle Lake from Pemetic Mountain in Acadia National Park

Have we ever so much as discovered and settled the shores? Let a man travel on foot along the coast . . . faithfully following the windings of every inlet and of every cape, and stepping to the music of the surf . . . and tell me if it looks like a discovered and settled country."

Henry David Thoreau

8

A bright October morning dawns below Otter Cliffs in Acadia National Park. Mount Desert Island, Maine.

WHITE MOUNTAINS, NEW HAMPSHIRE

New Hampshire's White Mountains are the loftiest mountains in the east; the tallest is 6,288-foot Mt. Washington.

Bombycilla cedrorum

—Cedar Waxwing—

10

Old Man of the Mountain

The "Old Man of the Mountain" is a series of five granite ledges 1,200 feet above Profile Lake. When viewed from a distance, the ledges resemble a craggy, human face in profile. Forty feet from chin to forehead, the profile was immortalized by Nathaniel Hawthorne's story "The Great Stone Face."

Men hang out their signs indicative of their respective trades: shoemakers hang out a gigantic shoe; jewelers, a monster watch . . . but up in the mountains of New Hampshire, God Almighty has hung out a sign to show that there He makes men.

Daniel Webster

The Profile House, a turn-of-the-century White Mountain resort, on land that is now Franconia Notch State Park

*Syringa
laciniata
-Lilac-*

The Flume, an 800-foot long natural gorge with granite walls that rise sixty to seventy feet straight up, was discovered in 1808 by ninety-three-year-old pioneer Aunt Jess Guernsey.

The Flume

*Betula papyrifera
-White Birch-*

11

The Cannon Mountain Aerial Tramway, the first of its kind in North America, opened in Franconia Notch in the summer of 1938 and carried almost seven million passengers before its retirement in 1980.

Cannon Mountain Aerial Tramway

In the woods, too, man casts off his years, as the snake his slough, and at what period soever of life is always a child. In the woods is perpetual youth. Within these plantations of God, a decorum and sanctity reign, a perennial festival is dressed, and the guest sees not how he should tire of them in a thousand years. In the woods, we return to reason and faith. There I feel nothing can befall me in life . . . my head bathed by the blithe air and uplifted into infinite space—all mean egotism vanishes.

Ralph Waldo Emerson

12

The magnificence of a New England autumn surrounds Silver Flume as it cascades through the forest of Crawford Notch State Park. White Mountains, New Hampshire.

CAPE COD, MASSACHUSETTS

Cape Cod is a narrow peninsula jutting out from Massachusetts into the Atlantic Ocean. It reaches thirty-five miles to the east, bends ninety degrees, and extends twenty miles to the north. In some places, the Cape is no more than a mile wide.

Gadus morhua
- Atlantic Cod -

English navigator Bartholomew Gosnold gave Cape Cod its name in 1602 when he observed the plentiful supply of cod in the waters off its shores.

14

Sailboats off Chatham, Cape Cod

Pluvialis squaterda
- Black-bellied Plover -

Countless species of migratory birds fly over the Cape as they travel north and south along the Atlantic flyway. Specific sightings depend upon the time of year; but bird watchers can find black-bellied plovers, sandpipers, greater yellowlegs, Canada geese, and other species on the beaches and in the forests of the Cape.

The beaches on the north side of the Cape are typical of those in the rest of New England; water temperatures rarely rise high enough for comfortable swimming. On the south side of the cape, however, the warm waters of the Gulf Stream create a more inviting surf.

Argopecten irradians

- Atlantic Bay Scallop -

Horshoe Crab

Many of the ponds on Cape Cod are the result of the retreating glaciers that left the area centuries ago. As the great ice sheets began to melt and creep slowly north, they left behind chunks of ice which became buried beneath gravel and other debris. When this ice melted, it left large depressions in the land which eventually filled with water and became ponds.

The horseshoe crab is found all along the beaches of Cape Cod. In truth, it is not a crab but a form of marine spider.

Cape Cod is covered by wet, marshy bogs that are fertile growing areas for azaleas, blueberries, and the region's number one crop, the cranberry.

15

Vaccinium macrocarpon

- Cranberry -

Boats pass through the waters of the Cape Cod Canal

*Most persons visit the seaside in
warm weather. . . . But I suspect
that the fall is the best season, for
then the atmosphere is more trans-
parent, and it is a greater pleasure
to look out over the sea.
In October, when the weather is not
intolerably cold, and the landscape
wears the autumnal tints, such
as . . . only a Cape Cod landscape
ever wears . . . that, I am
convinced, is the best time
to visit this shore.*

Henry David Thoreau

16

Wind and clouds announce a
summer storm off Coastguard Beach.
Cape Cod, Massachusetts.

ADIRONDACK MOUNTAINS, NEW YORK

The Adirondack Mountains stretch southwest from Lake Champlain in upstate New York. At their southern end, they are only 200 miles from New York City.

Gavia immer
— Common Loon —

The stately Grand View Hotel sits on the shore of Lake Placid, one of the larger of the Adirondack lakes

18

Forty-six Adirondack peaks approach or exceed 4,000 feet in height. Their slopes and valleys are covered with millions of acres of evergreen and hardwood forest, and more than 1,500 lakes are scattered at their feet.

Lonicera japonica

— Japanese Honeysuckle —

The highest point in the Adirondacks is Mt. Marcy, which stands 5,344 feet above sea level.

A beautiful resort welcomes travelers to Upper St. Regis Lake

Before roads cut through the thick forests of the Adirondacks, the best means of transportation was the Adirondack guide boat, a handmade, white cedar or white pine boat strong enough to carry two people and their gear yet light enough to be carried comfortably through the woods from waterway to waterway.

Man putting a canoe into St. Regis Lake

Oxalis montana
— *Common Wood Sorrel* —

Mirror Lake and Lake Placid with the Lake Placid Club buildings in foreground.

19

In 1894, the New York state constitution was amended to preserve the Adirondacks. The constitution now reads that the area "shall be forever kept as wild forest lands."

Gomphidius glutinosus
— *Slimy Gomphidius* —

Adirondack Park covers 9,375 square miles, an area almost three times as large as Yellowstone National Park and about equivalent to the state of New Hampshire.

It makes a man feel what it is to have all creation placed beneath his feet. There are woods there which it would take a lifetime to hunt over; mountains that seem shouldering each other, to boost the one whereon you stand up and away, heaven knows where. Thousands of little lakes are let in among them, so bright and clean that you would like to keep a canoe on each of them. Old Champlain, though fifty miles off, glistens below you like a strip of white birch bark, when slicked up by the moon on a frosty night; and the Green Mountains of Vermont beyond it fade and fade away, till they disappear as gradually as a cold scent when the dew rises.

John Cheney

The High Peaks Wilderness area is ablaze
with autumn color above Heart Lake.
Adirondack Mountains, New York

20

NIAGARA FALLS, NEW YORK

Niagara Falls consists of two separate falls, American Falls in New York and Horseshoe Falls in Ontario, Canada. Both falls are part of the Niagara River, which connects Lake Erie to Lake Ontario.

An early postcard depicts an aerial view of the two falls of Niagara

Lobelia Cardinalis

— Cardinal Flower —

22

In terms of power and volume of water, Niagara Falls is the third greatest waterfall in the world. Water plummets the 180 feet from the precipice at a rate of 700,000 gallons per second.

Water crashes over the edge of American Falls

American and Horseshoe Falls, 1905.

23

A railroad bridge spans the river above the Falls

Niagara Reservation State Park is the oldest existing state park in America. The park was established in order to save the falls from exploitation and commercialization and to preserve it as a truly natural wonder for future Americans. It was dedicated in July of 1885 with the promise that "from this hour, Niagara is free."

Rana palustris

— Pickerel Frog —

The craze for testing Niagara began in 1859 when French tightrope walker Blondin made a name for himself with his daring walks above the falls. His exploits drew other daredevils determined to conquer this natural wonder.

The golden sunshine tinged the sheets of the American cascade and painted on its heavy spray the broken semicircle of a rainbow, heaven's own beauty crowning earth's sublimity. My steps were slow, and I paused at every turn of the descent, as one lingers and pauses who discerns a brighter and brightening excellence in what he must soon behold no more. The solitude of the old wilderness now reigned over the whole vicinity of the falls. My enjoyment became the more rapturous because no poet shared it, nor wretch devoid of poetry profaned it; but the spot so famous throughout the world was all my own!

Nathaniel Hawthorne

24

A wall of water crashes over the falls
on the New York side.
Niagara Falls, New York

PICTURED ROCKS LAKESHORE, MICHIGAN

Pictured Rocks Lakeshore lies on the Lake Superior shore of Michigan's Upper Peninsula, where the cliffs, beaches, and sand dunes of the shoreline meet a dense, northern hardwood forest.

Glaucomys sabrinus
— Northern Flying Squirrel —

26

The colorful cliffs that give Pictured Rocks Lakeshore its name

Sable Falls in the forests of Pictured Rocks Lakeshore

The Pictured Rocks' cliffs rise to heights of 200 feet along a fifteen-mile stretch of the shore. Mineral deposits and organic matter create the colorful patterns that give the cliffs their name.

Monochamus scutellatus
— Black Pine Sawyer —

With the largest surface area of any freshwater lake in the world, Lake Superior produces enough moisture to generate up to 200 inches of snowfall annually.

A group of Pictured Rocks loggers in the late nineteenth century

27

The lumber from the great white pine forests that once stood along the shores of Lake Superior helped build the American Midwest. Between the years 1870 and 1900, Michigan produced more lumber than any other state in the nation.

A loggers' campsite on Lake Superior

Calypso bulbosa
— Calypso —

In early May, the floors of the forests surrounding the Lakeshore abound with violets, bloodroot, Dutchman's breeches, trout lily, and other colorful wildflowers. By June, however, the forest canopy has grown thick enough to block out the sunlight, and the beautiful flowers wither.

*I enter the woods as one
who goes to prayer
when the heart is full
and the need for consolation
is a cry.
I enter the woods with a hush
and stand where colonnades
of trees
lift vaulted branches over me. . . .
Here I partake of mystic
wine and bread;
my doubts uprooted
and my spirit fed.*

Elizabeth Peak

28

Early October sunshine reflects from
the waters of Munising Falls.
Pictured Rocks Lakeshore, Michigan

THE RADIANCE
OF THE
SOUTHEAST

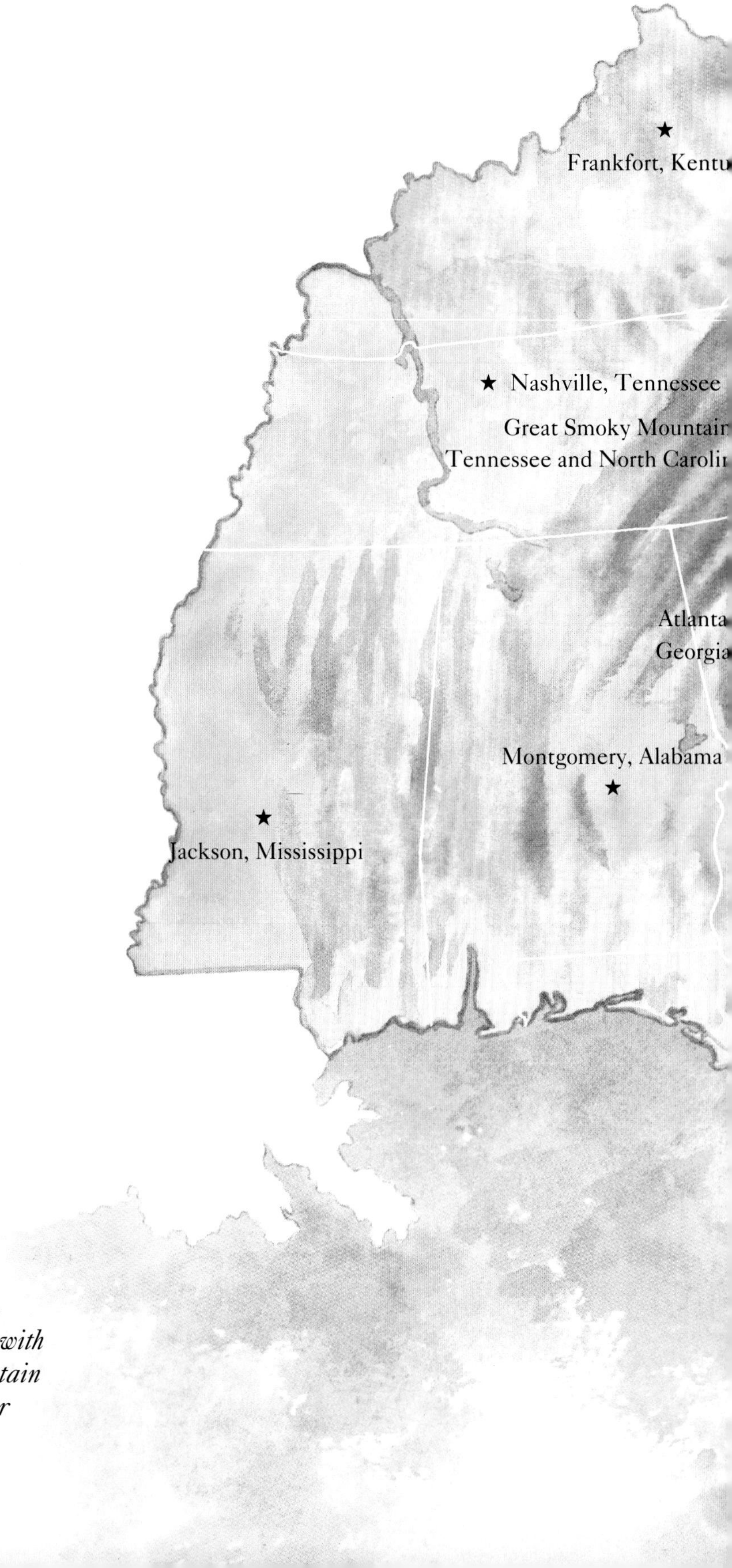

★ Frankfort, Kentu

★ Nashville, Tennessee

Great Smoky Mountain
Tennessee and North Carolir

Atlanta
Georgia

Montgomery, Alabama
★

★
Jackson, Mississippi

*Whether on long, white beaches filled with
a rainbow of birds or in lush, green mountain
groves carpeted with wildflowers, water
defines the beauty of the Southeast.*

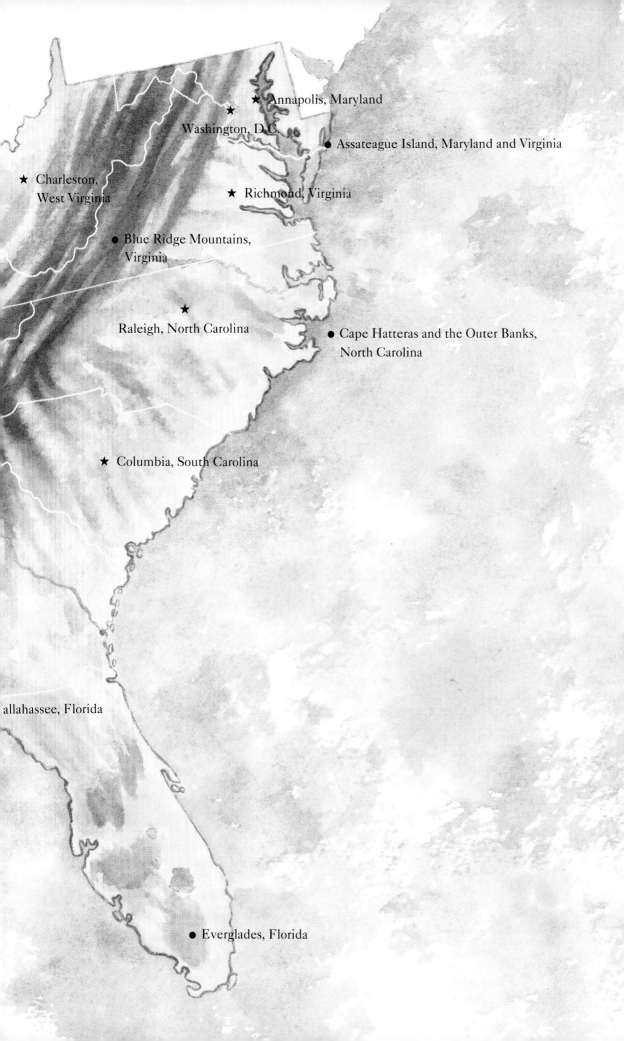

★ Annapolis, Maryland

★ Washington, D.C.

● Assateague Island, Maryland and Virginia

★ Charleston,
West Virginia

★ Richmond, Virginia

● Blue Ridge Mountains,
Virginia

★ Raleigh, North Carolina

● Cape Hatteras and the Outer Banks,
North Carolina

★ Columbia, South Carolina

allahassee, Florida

● Everglades, Florida

Assateague Island, Maryland, Virginia

Assateague Island is a thirty-seven-mile long barrier island that belongs to both Maryland and Virginia. The sand, wind, and waves that originally formed the island continue to shape its shoreline.

Lathyrus japonicus
— Beach Pea —

32

Assateague was a peninsula until a 1933 hurricane created an inlet at its northern end. Since that time, two jetties have been built to preserve Assateague as an island.

A lighthouse stands tall on Assateague Island

The sand on Assateague's beaches glitters, thanks to its ninety-percent quartz crystals.

Mellita sexiesperforata
— Six-hole Urchin —

The dunes of Assateague stretch into the horizon

An Assateague pony stallion

Assateague is home to two herds of wild ponies descended from domestic stock grazed in the area by seventeenth-century settlers. The settlers kept their ponies on the island to avoid the taxes and other restrictions of the mainland.

A pony mare and foal

On the Virginia end of the island lies Chincoteague National Wildlife Refuge, which was established in 1943 as a winter haven for migrating shorebirds. The island was purchased by the federal government with money raised through the sale of duck stamps.

Assateague is a favorite place for bird watchers, who can count on spotting an abundance of egrets, herons, tern, sandpipers, and gulls, as well as such rare species as the endangered piping plover.

A group of snow geese gathers in the waters off Assateague Island

charadrius melodus

-Piping Plover-

33

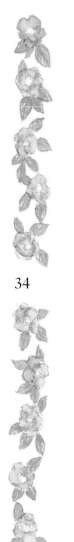

I wiped away
the weeds and foam;
I fetched my sea-born
treasures home.
But the poor, unsightly,
noisome things
Had left their beauty
on the shore
With the sun and the sand
and the wild uproar.

Ralph Waldo Emerson

34

Assateague ponies graze among the sand dunes.
Assateague Island, Virginia and Maryland

BLUE RIDGE MOUNTAINS, VIRGINIA

From Pennsylvania to North Carolina, the Blue Ridge Mountains stretch for 615 miles through western Virginia. To the west lies the Shenandoah Valley, to the east the Piedmont Plateau that leads to the Tidewater lowlands of coastal Virginia.

In the tragedies and other strains of our modern world, generations to come will receive a peace of mind and new hope uplifting their eyes to the peaks and canyons of Shenandoah National Park.

Harry F. Byrd, Sr.

Virginia governor and U. S. senator

36

Virginia's Natural Bridge, one of the world's wonders

The Blue Ridge are old mountains with smooth, sloping summits. Their peaks average between three and four thousand feet in height.

Spring brings a flourish of wildflowers to the Blue Ridge

Pheucticus ludovicianus

—Rose-breasted Grosbeak—

Two hundred species of birds inhabit the Blue Ridge Mountains; a day's walk through the forests will reveal as many as eighty different flowering plants.

The abundant population of black bears in the Blue Ridge hibernate during the long, harsh winters on the mountain slopes. They do, however, occasionally make an appearance during winter warm spells.

Vaccinium corymbosum

– Highbush Blueberry –

Sixty of the Blue Ridge peaks at the northern end of the range are part of Shenandoah National Park. Shenandoah, which means "Daughter of the Stars" in a local Indian tongue, is the name of a legendary river that runs just west of the Blue Ridge.

A black bear roams through the Blue Ridge forest

37

An old Virginia resort in the Blue Ridge

Trillium erectum

– Purple Trillium –

Hyla crucifer

– Spring Peeper –

In the nineteenth century, the large population of mountain farmers who cleared land for crops and pastures left the slopes of the Blue Ridge sparsely forested. Around the turn of the century, the farmers began to move out and allowed nature to reclaim its territory. Today, all but five percent of the Blue Ridge is reforested.

38

The groves were God's first temples. Ere man learned to hew the shaft and lay the architrave and spread the roof above them—ere he framed the lofty vault to gather and roll back the sound of anthems; in the darkling wood, amid the cool and silence, he knelt down and offered to the Mightiest solemn thanks.

William Cullen Bryant

A thick fog rises over Cumberland Gap
on a picture-perfect autumn day.
Blue Ridge Mountains , Virginia

CAPE HATTERAS AND THE OUTER BANKS, NORTH CAROLINA

anas platyrhynchos

—Mallard—

The Outer Banks are three barrier islands located off the North Carolina coast. Cape Hatteras is found near the center of the Outer Banks on Hatteras Island.

Salicornia

—Glasswort—

Snow geese, Canada geese, and countless waterfowl rest along the beaches of Cape Hatteras during their long fall and spring migrations. The birds are protected at Pea Island National Wildlife Refuge on Hatteras Island.

40

History is preserved at Lane's Fort in the Fort Raleigh National Historic Site on the Outer Banks

The Wright brothers' historic first flight took place in 1903 at Kill Devil Hills, located on Bodie Island, the northernmost island of the Outer Banks.

Cape Hatteras Lighthouse

41

In 1870, the Cape Hatteras Lighthouse stood 1,500 feet from the sea; by 1989, erosion had left the North Carolina landmark only 200 feet from the Atlantic's waters.

Quercus virginiana

– Live Oak –

Ocypode quadrata

– Ghost Crab –

On high, protected areas of the Outer Banks, forests of oak and cedar grow much as they do on the mainland. The dwarfed, oddly-shaped trees that grow closer to the shore are more typical of the islands' vegetation that is transformed by the relentless force of the salt-laden winds.

The peaceful atmosphere of the Outer Banks contrasts greatly with some of the more treacherous waters in the Atlantic just off the islands' shores. Since the first Europeans settled the area, 600 ships have wrecked along the hidden sand shoals beneath the sea.

Donax variabilis

– Coquina Shell –

Even as a boy, I had the fancy, the wish, to write a piece, perhaps a poem, about the seashore—that suggesting, dividing line, contact, junction, the solid marrying the liquid— that curious, lurking something . . . which means far more than its mere first sight, grand as that is—blending the real and the ideal, and each made a portion of the other.

Walt Whitman

42

The Cape Hatteras Lighthouse rises starkly above the sparse vegetation of the island's shore. Cape Hatteras and the Outer Banks, North Carolina

GREAT SMOKY MOUNTAINS, TENNESSEE, NORTH CAROLINA

The Great Smoky Mountains are part of the Appalachian Mountains. They run along the Tennessee-North Carolina border, equidistant from Asheville, North Carolina, and Knoxville, Tennessee.

Tamias striatus
—Eastern Chipmunk—

44

The "smoke" that gives these mountains their name is the result of vast amounts of vapor emitted by the dense, rich forest cover.

Chimney Tops, Great Smoky Mountains National Park

Uvularia sessifolia
—Sessile Bellwort—

The Smoky Mountains are among the oldest mountains on the earth; their smooth, rounded peaks are the result of countless years of slow erosion. At one time, the Smoky Mountains probably resembled the jagged, rocky peaks of our western mountains.

Boletus edulis
—King Bolete—

View of the Smoky Mountains from Clingman's Dome

The tallest point in the Smoky Mountains is Clingman's Dome, which rises 6,642 feet above sea level. In all, twenty of the range's peaks rise to 6,000 feet or more.

The elevation of the mountains makes the forest appear more like the forests of New England than like other forests in the South. The most common trees in the Smoky Mountains are red spruce and fraser fir.

Thirteen hundred varieties of flowering plants grow in the forests of the Smoky Mountains. More then 200 different birds can be seen and heard in the region.

An old cabin in the Smoky Mountain forest

Rhododendron catawbiense

— Catawba Rhododendron —

Rhododendron bushes flourish on the hill-sides of the mountains. In some places they grow in impenetrable clusters, with individual bushes reaching heights of twenty feet.

Halisidota maculata

— Spotted Tiger Moth —

Cades Cove, a broad valley surrounded by mountains, is preserved evidence of the Smoky Mountains' past. Its pastures, farmhouses, churches, and cemeteries all bear witness to the not-too-distant time when the Smokies were filled with small farming communities.

45

*It was the vastness of the view, the
nearly unbroken surface of
verdure, that contained the
principle of grandeur. The beauty
was to be traced in the delicate
tints, relieved by gradations of
light and shadow; while the solemn
repose induced the feeling
allied to awe.*

46

James Fenimore Cooper

The late summer afternoon sun shines over
the vast, green expanse of the mountain tops.
Great Smoky Mountains, Tennessee

EVERGLADES, FLORIDA

The Everglades is actually one broad, shallow river that runs southward from Lake Okeechobee in central Florida into Florida Bay. Native Americans called the area *Pa-hay-okee*, which means "river of grass."

malaclemys terrapin
- Diamondback Terrapin -

Deep in the Florida Everglades

The beauty of the Florida Everglades

Sawgrass growing in the water covers the majority of the Everglades. The watery prairie is occasionally interrupted by small rises—no more than ten feet in height—which support pine groves, ponds full of bald cypress, and dense mangrove forests.

epiphyte
-Wild Pine-

48

Egrets congregate along the banks of the Everglades

49

Herons, pelicans, spoonbills, and more than 300 other species of birds attract the greatest number of visitors to the Everglades.

Trichechus manatus
— Manatee —

ajaia ajaia

— Roseate Spoonbill —

Here are no lofty peaks seeking the sky, no mighty glaciers or rushing streams. . . . Here is land, tranquil in its quiet beauty, serving not as the source of water but as the last receiver of it.

President Harry S. Truman

Collops nigriceps
— Flower Beetle —

The Everglades is the final sanctuary for some of Florida's endangered species. The Florida panther, crocodiles, and the manatee, an air-breathing, vegetarian sea cow, all find security within the boundaries of the Everglades.

There are no other Everglades in the world. They are, they always have been, one of the unique regions of the earth, remote, never wholly known. Nothing anywhere else is like them: their vast, glittering openness, wider than the enormous visible round of the horizon, the racing free saltness and sweetness of the massive winds, under the dazzling blue height of space. . . . The miracle of the light pours over the green and brown expanse of sawgrass and of water, shining and slow-moving below, the grass and the water that is the meaning and the central fact of the Everglades.

Marjory Stoneman Douglas

50

Lush undergrowth and cypress trees
flourish along the water's edge.
Everglades, Florida

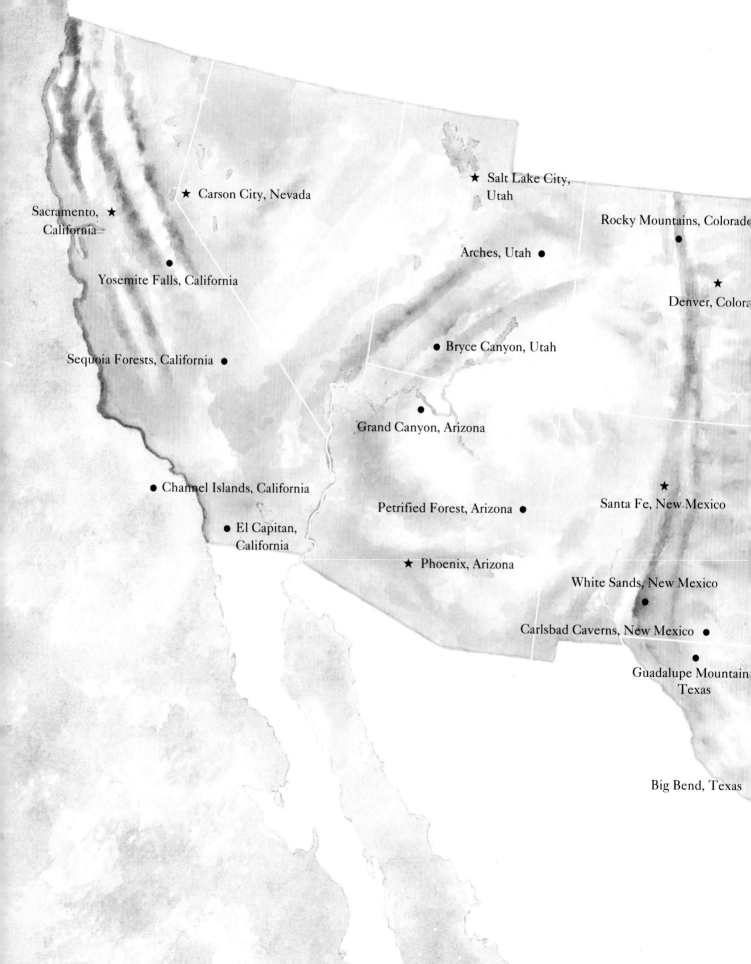

★ Salt Lake City, Utah

★ Carson City, Nevada

Rocky Mountains, Colorado ●

Sacramento, California ★

Arches, Utah ●

★ Denver, Colorado

Yosemite Falls, California ●

Bryce Canyon, Utah ●

Sequoia Forests, California ●

Grand Canyon, Arizona ●

Channel Islands, California ●

Petrified Forest, Arizona ●

★ Santa Fe, New Mexico

El Capitan, California ●

★ Phoenix, Arizona

White Sands, New Mexico ●

Carlsbad Caverns, New Mexico ●

Guadalupe Mountains, Texas ●

Big Bend, Texas

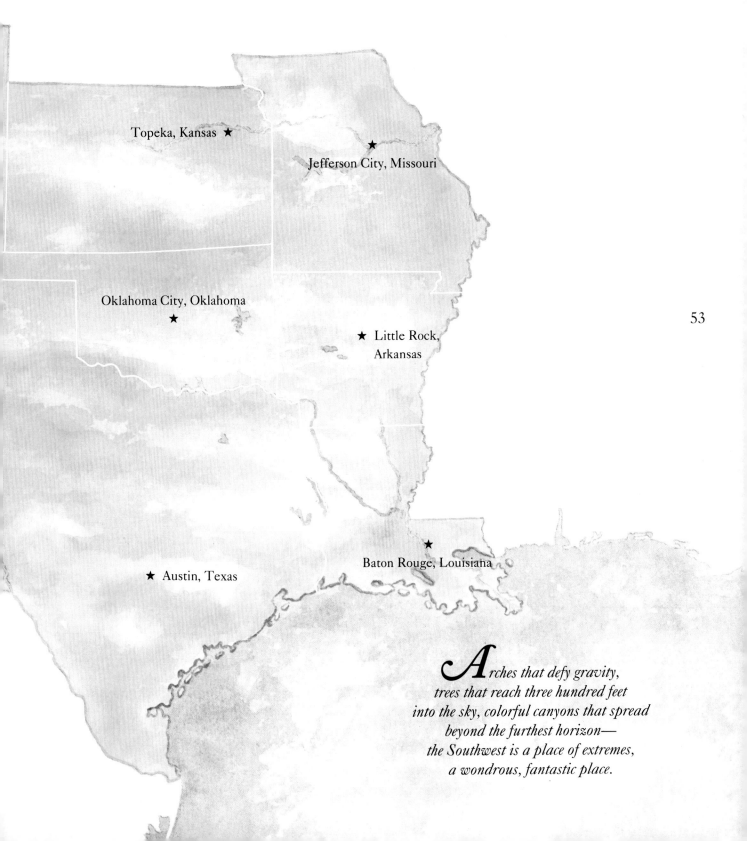

Topeka, Kansas ★

★ Jefferson City, Missouri

Oklahoma City, Oklahoma
★

53

★ Little Rock,
Arkansas

★ Baton Rouge, Louisiana

★ Austin, Texas

*A*rches that defy gravity,
*trees that reach three hundred feet
into the sky, colorful canyons that spread
beyond the furthest horizon—
the Southwest is a place of extremes,
a wondrous, fantastic place.*

BIG BEND, TEXAS

Big Bend, Texas, lies along the border of Mexico within the curve of the Rio Grande River.

Kallstoemia grandiflora

— Desert Poppy —

The Basin in the Chisos Mountains

Thousands of years ago, Big Bend was an inland sea, not a desert. As the seas began to dry, the area became a series of marshes and tropical forests. These marshes were home to the largest flying creature ever known—the pterosaur, or pterodactyl. Fossils reveal that the now-extinct bird had a wingspan of thirty-eight feet.

54

The colorful, castle-like Casa Grande in the Chisos Mountains

A postcard view of Emory Peak in the Chisos Mountains

Today, about ninety-eight percent of Big Bend is desert. The remaining land consists of the Rio Grande River and the Chisos Mountains, whose rocky cliffs rise dramatically from the desert floor.

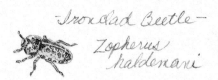

— Ironclad Beetle —
Zopherus haldemani

The highest point in Big Bend is 7,835-foot Emory Peak, which offers a dramatic view across the desert to the Rio Grande.

Countless migrating birds, including the Colima warbler, a Mexican bird found nowhere else in the United States, make their summer homes in the Chisos Mountains. The banks of the Rio Grande River are also teeming with bird life. Four hundred species depend on the river and the life along its banks for their livelihood.

Lepus californicus

—Black-tailed Jack Rabbit—

The century plant flourishes in Big Bend's desert. It lives for up to fifty years as a dense rosette of spiny leaves before sending a thick stalk fifteen feet straight up into the air.

55

Agave parryi

—Parry's Century Plant—

The roadrunner, a member of the cuckoo family, thrives in the Texas desert. This bird can cover ground at a speed of fifteen miles per hour in pursuit of food.

Lower Window Falls inside Big Bend National Park

Geococcyx californianus

—Greater Roadrunner—

Nature is not benevolent; nature is just, gives pound for pound, measure for measure, makes no exceptions, never tempers her decrees with mercy, or winks at any infringement of her laws. And in the end is not this best? . . . It is a hard gospel; but rocks are hard too, yet they form the foundations of the hills.

John Burroughs

56

Prickly pear cacti decorate the
volcanic rock of Goat Mountain.
Big Bend, Texas

GUADALUPE MOUNTAINS, TEXAS

The Guadalupe Mountains are the remains of an ancient ocean reef stranded in the flats of northwestern Texas, near the New Mexico border. After the sea dried and disappeared, movement beneath the earth's surface raised the reef to create a range of sheer limestone peaks.

Crotaphytus collaris

— Collard Lizard —

58

The rocky peaks of the Guadalupe Mountains

Guadalupe Peak, at 8,749 feet, is the highest point in the Guadalupes and the highest point in Texas. More dramatic, however, is El Capitan, whose 8,085-foot rise includes a 2,000-foot sheer limestone cap.

Apiomerus

— Bee Assassin —

Deep canyons protected from the desert heat are found throughout the Guadalupes. The canyons offer underground springs to help plant and animal life flourish within the desert mountains.

Guiraca
caerulea

-Blue
Grosbeak-

In September 1858, an eastbound stage met a westbound stage at the Pinery Stagecoach Station deep in the Guadalupes for an exchange of mail. This was the first transcontinental mail exchange in American history.

The Pinery Stagecoach Station

59

An aerial view of the Guadalupe Mountains

Opuntia
polyacantha

-Plains Pricklypear-

The hills and gulleys bore the appearance of having been created by some vast, fierce torrent . . . as if nature had saved all her ruggedness to pile it up in this colossal form.

Reporter Walter Ormsby, passenger on the first stage to stop at the Pinery

*My heart is awed within me
when I think of the great miracle
that still goes on,
in silence, round me—
the perpetual work
of Thy creation, finished, yet
renewed forever.
Written on Thy works
I read the lesson of
Thy own eternity.*

William Cullen Bryant

60

The sandstone boulders of the mountains
reflect the last rays of a March sunset.
Guadalupe Mountains, Texas

CARLSBAD CAVERNS, NEW MEXICO

Carlsbad Caverns began as chambers in the same reef that formed the Guadalupe Mountains. As the earth's surface raised the mountains skyward, the chambers were pushed into southeastern New Mexico, adjacent to the Texas border.

The cars of early tourists fill the parking lot at Carlsbad Caverns

62

A group of tourists inside Kings Palace, 1914

Typhlichthys Subterraneus

Mineral-carrying water dripping from the caves' ceilings forms the spires called stalagmites that grow upward from the cave floors. Stalactites, formed by the same water, grow down from the ceiling in the same shapes.

Tarida brasiliensis

- Mexican free-tail Bat -

Four hundred thousand bats make their daytime home in Bat Cave; they fly out each night at a rate of 5000 per minute to feed on insects. The spectacle of the bats' nightly flight led to the discovery of Carlsbad Caverns.

63

Visitors in Guano Bucket on 170-foot descent into bat cave portion of Carlsbad Cavern in 1924

During the first few years following its discovery, visitors to Carlsbad Caverns were lowered 200 feet to the cave's floor in miners' buckets.

The Caverns' largest room is the size of fourteen football fields; its deepest room sinks 1,013 feet below the earth's surface.

64

The great cave is not
merely a spectacle to the eye;
it is a wonder to the ear,
a strangeness to the smell
and to the touch.
The body feels the presence
of unusual conditions
through every pore.

John Burroughs

The spectacular interiors of the great caves
awe thousands of visitors each year.
Carlsbad Caverns, New Mexico

WHITE SANDS, NEW MEXICO

New Mexico's White Sands, located in the Tularosa Basin in the south-central part of the state, are the world's largest deposit of gypsum dunes. The field of dunes is thirty miles long and ten miles wide. Gypsum is the same mineral used to make plaster of Paris.

Sonora semiannulata
—Ground Snake —

66

Museum and Cactus Garden at entrance to White Sands National Monument

White Sands gypsum comes from the San Andres Mountains to the west and the Sacramento Mountains to the east. Rain and melting snow carry the gypsum deposits to the White Sands basin.

Piranga
ludoviciana
—Western Tanager—

As the wind blows, the dunes of
White Sands are constantly reshaped;
they shift more than thirty feet in an
average year.

atriplex
canescens

– Four-wing saltbush –

Two hardy plants, the yucca and the
saltbush, have adapted over centuries
to learn to make frugal use of the limited moisture available in order to survive in this dry, white desert.

67

An ancient Native American village in New Mexico

*– Cactus
Mouse –*

*Peromyscus
eremicus*

Most of the rodents and lizards living
in White Sands have developed
white coats or white skin as
camouflage.

The long line of dunes . . . are
just as desolate,
yet they are wonderfully beautiful.
The desert sand is finer than snow,
and its curves and arches . . .
are as graceful as the lines
of running water.
The dunes are always rhythmical
and flowing in their forms;
and for color the desert has
nothing that surpasses them . . .
under a blue moonlight they
shine white as icebergs
in the northern seas.

John Charles Van Dyke

68

Yuccas provide a splash of color between
the sparkling white sand and the fluffy
white clouds on a March afternoon.
White Sands, New Mexico

PETRIFIED FOREST, ARIZONA

The Petrified Forest is located on the high plateaus of northeastern Arizona's Painted Desert, a barren region of buttes, hills, gullies, and limited vegetation.

Tourists walk beneath the painted hills of Chinle Formation

The colorful logs and branches that now lie scattered in the Petrified Forest were once giant pine and sequoia trees. The forces of nature have transformed the wood into beautiful, rainbow-colored rock.

Prosopis pubescens
— Screwbean Mesquite —

Stumps of petrified wood

70

An artist's rendering of the Triassic period in the Petrified Forest

The trees of the Petrified Forest resemble wood, but they have taken on an entirely new identity. Hard enough to scratch glass, the transformed wood is dense and heavy, weighing up to 200 pounds per cubic foot.

Natiosorex crawfordi
— Desert Shrew —

Years ago, Native Americans living in the Petrified Forest area made tools and arrowheads from the smaller pieces of wood; large stumps and logs were fashioned into houses. The wood, unknown outside the region, was also valuable for trading.

- *Indian Blanket* -   *Gaillardia pulchella*

The American public first learned of the Petrified Forest in the mid-1800s when Army mappers and surveyors returned from their travels with stories of a "painted desert and its trees turned to stone."

The Painted Desert

A walk through the colorful hills of the Petrified Forest

71

Every state in the country contains petrified wood, but Arizona's Petrified Forest contains the highest concentration of petrified wood in the world. Tourists, souvenir hunters, and gem collectors—all eager to make a fortune collecting and selling the beautiful, jewel-like wood—nearly destroyed the Arizona forest shortly after its discovery. Today, the area is protected from souvenir hunters and collectors.

amphispiza bilineata
- *Black Throated Sparrow* -

72

*Chips of carnelian,
onyx, agate, and jasper
were strewn . . . in exotic
and intricate patterns
like a kaleidoscope
fashioned by
God's hands.*

John Muir

Ancient trees are forever preserved as
giant gems through centuries of fossilization.
Petrified Forest, Arizona

GRAND CANYON, ARIZONA

The Grand Canyon, carved slowly and steadily by the Colorado River, dominates the northwestern Arizona landscape. By river, the journey through the canyon is 277 miles.

Hyles lineata
—White-lined Sphinx—

The Grand Canyon Bridge over the Colorado River

The distance between the Grand Canyon's walls varies greatly. At the canyon's narrowest point, the walls open a gorge of less than a half mile. At its widest point, the Grand Canyon lives up to its name, spreading a full eighteen miles from rim to rim. One central section of the canyon plunges an incredible mile from rim to floor.

74

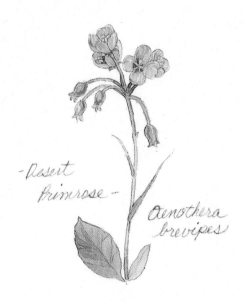

—Desert Primrose—
Oenothera brevipes

At the canyon's North Rim, 8,803 foot-high Point Imperial offers the highest view of the chasm. Because the land slopes to the south, the canyon's South Rim is 1,200 feet lower than the North Rim.

Artist Thomas Moran sketching on the rim of the canyon

The Colorado River continues to shape the Grand Canyon as it carries an average of 400,000 tons of silt each day through the canyon.

Hyla arenicolor
– Canyon Treefrog –

Explorer John Wesley Powell called the Grand Canyon "the most sublime spectacle on the earth."

Out on the rim of the Grand Canyon

75

A group descends Bright Angel Trail on mules, 1902

Opuntia
basilaris
– Beavertail Cactus –

Do nothing to mar its grandeur. Keep it for your children, and your children's children, and all who come after you, as the one great sight which every American should see.

President Theodore Roosevelt

The magnitude of the chasm, however, is by no means the most impressive element of its character; nor is the inner gorge the most impressive of its constituent parts. The thoughtful mind is far more deeply moved by the splendor and grace of Nature's architecture. Forms so new . . . cannot indeed be appreciated after the study of a single hour or day.

Clarence Dutton

76

The awesome beauty of the Grand Canyon
offers a spectacular view from the south rim
between Yavapai and Mather Points.
Grand Canyon, Arizona

Sequoia Forests, California

The great Sequoia Forests stand in the Sierra Nevada mountain range in the central part of California. The Sierra Nevada is the highest American mountain range outside of Alaska; the range's greatest peak, Mt. Whitney, stands 14,495 feet above sea level.

"The Four Guardsmen" of Sequoia National Park

78

A horse-drawn carriage drives between two giant sequoia trees

Approximately seventy-five groves of sequoia trees grow on the western slopes of the Sierra Nevada at elevations between 3,500 and 7,500 feet.

Hygrophorus speciosus
– Larch Waxy Cap –

The trees in California are remnants of forests that once spread across much of the northern hemisphere. Scientists believe that some of the trees in the area are more than 2,000 years old.

Ariolimax columbianus
– Banana Slug –

The General Sherman tree is almost 300 feet high and weighs 4,500,000 pounds. It is the world's largest living thing. If this giant tree were chopped down today, its wood could build forty homes. Each year it adds growth equivalent to a sixty-foot tree.

Cars and tourists on the Auto Log, a fallen sequoia transformed into a roadway

The sequoia is related to the redwood, which grows near the ocean,
not on inland mountain slopes.
Although the redwood is the world's
tallest tree, it is relatively slender in
comparison with the sequoia. The
trunks of the great sequoia are as
thick as thirty-two feet in diameter at
their bases.

*Tamiasciurus
douglassi*

- Douglas' Squirrel -

The chickaree squirrel plays an
important role in the life cycle of the
sequoia. In a year, an average squirrel
cuts down and breaks open 3200
cones, which release the seeds that
will become the next generation of
sequoias.

79

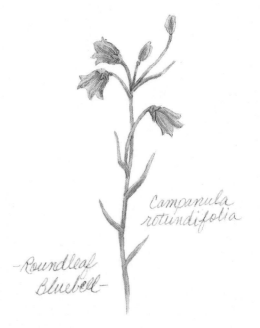

*Campanula
rotundifolia*

*-Roundleaf
Bluebell-*

No sequoia tree has ever died of old
age. Their fatal weakness, however,
is their root system, which is buried
only four feet under the ground.
These shallow roots spread out to
100 feet and provide a precarious
anchor for the giant trees they support.

*The sunshine falls in glory
through the colossal spires
and crowns,
each a symbol of
health and strength,
the noble shafts faithfully upright
like pillars of temples,
upholding a roof of infinite, leafy,
interlacing arches
and fretted skylights.*

John Muir

80

The General Sherman rises dramatically
from the forest floor toward the sky.
Sequoia Forests, California

CHANNEL ISLANDS, CALIFORNIA

The Channel Islands lie between ten and seventy miles off the southern California coast; the eight islands are actually mountains stranded at sea; the four northernmost islands are an extension of the Santa Monica Mountains.

Pelecanus accidentalis
— Brown Pelican —

82

A visitor among the wildflowers on the Channel Islands

Coreopsis lanceolata

— Lance-leaved Coreopsis —

Due to the lack of fresh water on the islands, plant growth is limited to shrubs and other low-growing plants. Nonetheless, yellow coreopsis, white morning glories, gold fields, and other beautiful wildflowers flourish alongside the dunes and rocky cliffs each spring.

Cuyler Harbor, Channel Isalnds, California

Gray whales stop at the Channel Islands on their yearly 5,000-mile migration from the Arctic to Baja, California. These giant whales weigh up to twenty tons and are forty-five feet in length.

83

Eschrichtius robustus
- Gray Whale -

Anacapa Island is host to the only permanent colony of brown pelicans on the West Coast. After near extinction, these birds are just returning to the area.

San Miguel Island is host to the most varied collection of seals found anywhere in the world; they mate and rear their young on the island each year. The Channel Islands are the only breeding colony of northern fur seals south of Alaska.

Callorhinus
ursinus

- Northern Fur Seal -

*C*limb the mountains
and get their good tidings.
Nature's peace will flow into you
as sunshine flows into trees.
The winds will blow
their own freshness unto you,
and the storms, their energy,
while cares will drop off like
autumn leaves.

John Muir

84

A February sunrise warms the stark peaks
amid the cold water of the Pacific Ocean.
Channel Islands, California

YOSEMITE FALLS, CALIFORNIA

Located in Yosemite Valley in the Sierra Nevada of central California, Yosemite Falls is one of many striking water features in an area known as "the place of dancing waters."

Colias alexandra
—Queen Alexandra's Sulpher—

86

The cascading waters of Yosemite Falls

The High Sierras from Glacier Point, Yosemite Valley

More than half of the country's highest waterfalls are found in Yosemite Valley. Yosemite Falls is the highest waterfall in North America and the second highest in the world. Its two cascades plunge a total of 2,425 feet, equivalent to thirteen Niagara Falls.

Argia violacea
—Violet Tail—

The most songful streams, the noblest forests, the loftiest granite domes, the deepest ice-sculptured canyons, and snowy mountains soaring into the sky.

John Muir

The Yosemite area is home to seventy-five species of mammals, 220 varieties of birds, twenty-five distinct reptiles, and 1200 flowering plants.

Vulpes vulpes

-Red Fox-

Ribes cereum

-Wax Currant-

87

Wawona Tunnel Tree in Yosemite Valley

The Sierra Club, founded by John Muir, dedicated its early efforts to securing federal control of the Yosemite region.

sequoiadendron giganteum

-Giant Sequoia-

I know of no single owner of nature on earth which can claim a superiority over the Yosemite.

Horace Greely

California Redwood Highway

*It is the upper and highest cataract
that is most wonderful to the eye, as
well as most musical.
The cliff is so sheer that there is
no break in the body of the water
during the whole of its descent
of more than a quarter of a mile. It
pours in a curve from the
summit . . . to the basin
that hoards it but a moment
for the cascades that follow.
And what endless complexities
and opulence of beauty in the forms
and motions of the cataract!*

Starr King

88

A late afternoon fog settles over a spectacular and
inspirational view of the Yosemite Valley.
Yosemite Falls, California

EL CAPITAN, CALIFORNIA

Located within Yosemite Valley, El Capitan is the world's largest solid granite rock, rising 3,604 feet above the Merced River.

Hyla regilla

— Pacific Treefrog —

90

The Yosemite Valley contains the world's largest collection of granite domes. In fact, instead of a series of individual peaks, the entire Sierra Nevada mountain range is one block of solid granite raised by the forces of the earth and carved and shaped by glaciers.

Half Dome overlooking the Merced River

Iris tenax

— Tough-leaved Iris —

Clarkia amoena

— Farewell to Spring —

It was like lying in a great, solemn cathedral, far vaster and more beautiful than any built by the hand of man.

President Theodore Roosevelt speaking after a camping trip to Yosemite Valley

The beauty of Yosemite

91

Oreortyx pictus

— Mountain Quail —

In addition to the granite domes and waterfalls, Yosemite Valley is also home to the world's oldest sequoia tree, the Grizzly Giant, the fifth largest tree in the world.

Yosemite Falls can be seen from El Capitan

There are falls of water elsewhere finer; there are more stupendous rocks. . . . It is in no scene or scenes the charm consists, but in the miles of scenery where cliffs of awful height and rocks of vast magnitude and of varied and exquisite coloring, and banked and fringed and draped and shadowed by the tender foliage of noble and lovely trees and bushes, reflected from the most placid pools, and associated with the most tranquil meadows, the most playful streams, and every variety of soft and peaceful pastoral beauty. The union of the deepest sublimity with the deepest beauty of nature . . . constitutes the Yosemite, the greatest glory of nature.

Frederick Law Olmstead

92

The sheer facade of El Capitan rises above
the Merced River on a winter afternoon.
El Capitan, California

BRYCE CANYON, UTAH

Countless small canyons enclosed in one large canyon constitute Bryce Canyon in southern Utah. The canyon began as a plateau raised by pressure within the earth. Over the years, rivers and streams eroded the plateau and left the strange rock formations now known as Bryce Canyon.

Thor's Hammer and the Temple of Oriris

The magnificence of Bryce Canyon dsisplayed in a formation known as Fairyland

94

Bryce's rainbow of colors is the result of mineral deposits. Layers of different types of rock create the pink, red, orange, white, gold, purple, and blue stripes that ring the canyon walls.

*Athene cunicularia
—Burrowing Owl—*

At the southern rim of Bryce Canyon is Rainbow Point, the canyon's highest point. At 9,105 feet above sea level, Rainbow Point provides a stunning view of the intricate rock formations within the canyon.

Ponderosa Pine.

Pinus ponderosa

Great forests of ponderosa pine grow to heights of 100 feet at the high elevations of the canyon's southern rim. Below the rim, as the terrain gradually changes from thick, shady forest to parched desert, ponderosa pine give way to the more rugged pinyon pine.

Snow on Silent City

A rock arch carved by the forces of water, wind, and time

95

Bryce Canyon National Park takes its name from an early settler named Ebenezer Bryce, who tried unsuccessfully to raise cattle on the land. He called the canyon that would eventually bear his name "a heck of a place to lose a cow."

Tribulus terrestris

—Puncture Vine—

Time, geologic time,
looks out at us from the rocks
as no other objects
in the landscape.
The youth of the earth
is in the soil
and in the trees and verdure
that spring from it;
its age is in the rocks.

John Burroughs

96

An October morning reveals the spectacular
formations rising near Sunset Point.
Bryce Canyon, Utah

ARCHES, UTAH

Southeastern Utah boasts the greatest number of natural rock arches in the world. More than 200 in number, the arches range from three to 300 feet in width.

Battarrea phalloides

— Desert Stalked Puffball —

Wind and water erosion combined with the shifting salt and sand under the earth's surface to form the arches over long periods of time.

At the rim of a canyon, Delicate Arch stands sixty-five feet high and thirty-five feet wide. Area cowboys knew this landmark as the Schoolmarm's Bloomers.

98

The Double "O" Arch

Landscape Arch

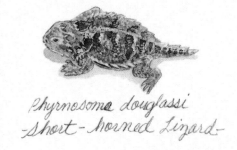

Phyrnosoma douglassi — Short-horned Lizard —

Landscape Arch is 291 feet wide and 106 feet high. Continuing erosion, however, threatens its existence—at one point, it is now only six feet thick.

Pinyon pines flourish among the arches. These rugged trees reach maturity in 200 years, although they grow to only twenty feet in height.

Pinus edulis

- Colorado Pinyon -

The Three Gossips

A balanced rock sits atop a spire

Phlox longifolia

- Long-leaved Phlox -

Wildflowers adapt to the harsh desert by living quickly. They bloom in profusion in the mild, rainy months of April and May and then disappear for another year.

Utah's arches are located on the Northern Colorado Plateau that also includes the Grand Canyon, the Petrified Forest, and Mesa Verde.

100

Perhaps no portion of the earth's surface is more irremediably sterile, none more hopelessly lost to human occupation. . . . The surface was diversified by columns, spires, castles, and battlement towers of colossal but often beautiful proportions, closely resembling elaborate structures of art, but in effect far surpassing the most imposing monuments of human skill.

J.S. Newberry

Delicate Arch, a monument to the wonder of nature's beauty, stands on the rim of a canyon. Arches, Utah

ROCKY MOUNTAINS, COLORADO

The Rocky Mountains are part of the 10,000-mile-long Continental Divide that runs from Alaska to Patagonia in South America. All of the mountains in Canada and the United States that lie along this divide are part of the Rocky Mountain range.

West from the summit of Pike's Peak

102

On the Big Circle Trip via Ute Pass Highway to Cripple Creek

In the Rockies, every 1000-foot rise in elevation is equivalent to straight northward travel of 350 miles. The mile-and-a-quarter trip from the lowest valley to the highest peak is comparable to a journey of 2000 miles to the north, with all the corresponding changes in climate, flora, and fauna.

Dendroica townsendi

— Townsend's Warbler —

Above the 11,000-foot tree line, alpine tundra covers the Rockies. Tundra plants are specially adapted to survive in the harsh alpine environment, but they are also very delicate. A three-inch-high plant may be over 200 years old; but if it is crushed by hikers' feet, it may take a century to restore itself.

Cassiope mertensiana

-White Mountain-heather-

103

Pike's Peak Avenue

Car at Inspiration Point

Pike's Peak is named for Zebulon Pike, one of the first American explorers to see the Rocky Mountains. Pike's effort to reach the summit of the peak was a failure.

At 14,255 feet above sea level, Long's Peak is the highest point in Rocky Mountain National Park.

More than 100 peaks located within the boundaries of Rocky Mountain National Park are over 12,000 feet high.

From one hundred miles distant,
out on the plains
of Colorado or Wyoming,
these snowy, rugged
mountain tops give one a thrill
as they appear to join
with the clouds
and form a horizon
that seems to be
a part of the scenery
of the sky.

Enos Mill

104

The Maroon Bells rise behind
Maroon Lake in Aspen, Colorado.
Rocky Mountains, Colorado

Olympia, Washington
★

● Mt. Ranier, Washington

★ Salem, Oregon

● Crater Lake, Oregon

★ Boise, Idaho

● Glacier National Park,
Montana

★ Helena, Montana

Grand Canyon of Yellowstor
Wyoming
●
● Old Faithful, Wyoming
● Grand Tetons,
Wyoming

THE ALLURE
OF THE
NORTHWEST

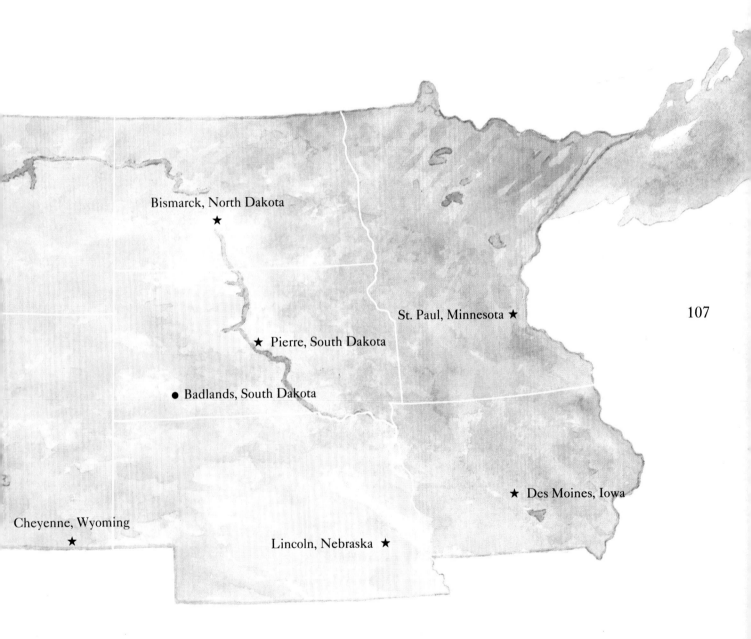

Bismarck, North Dakota
★

St. Paul, Minnesota ★

★ Pierre, South Dakota

● Badlands, South Dakota

★ Des Moines, Iowa

Cheyenne, Wyoming
★

Lincoln, Nebraska ★

107

*The Northwest is a region of jagged
mountain peaks and towering, steaming
geysers, a place where glaciers still shape
the landscape and volcanoes
rumble forebodingly.*

CRATER LAKE, OREGON

Crater Lake is located in southern Oregon at the sunken summit of Mt. Mazama, part of the majestic Cascade Range.

A postcard view of Crater Lake, Oregon

The steep rim slopes down to Crater Lake

Epilobium angustifolium

- Fireweed -

After a violent eruption, Mt. Mazama lost its inner structure and collapsed in on itself, leaving a basin-shaped depression at the top of the volcano. Water from rain and snow filled the caldera to create Crater Lake.

108

Chalceria rubidus

Crater Lake is 1,932 feet deep and covers an area of twenty square miles. It is the deepest lake in the country, the second deepest in the western hemisphere, and the seventh deepest in the world.

The clear blue waters of Crater Lake

The Phantom Ship, a rock island rising from the waters of Crater Lake

The lake is one of the clearest in the world. The Secchi Disk, an eight-inch, circular, black and white disk used to measure water clarity, remains visible 120 feet below the lake's surface.

A fresh snowfall at Crater Lake

*Marmota flaviventris
—Yellow-bellied Marmot—*

The average annual snowfall at Crater Lake is fifty feet. July and August are the only months when the rim of the lake is not covered with snow.

Crater Lake was discovered in 1853 by John Wesley Hillman, a miner searching for the Lost Cabin Mine. The discovery was not made public, however, for thirty-one years. Crater Lake National Park was established in May 1902.

*Pinus monticola
—Western
White Pine—*

*A lake is the landscape's
most beautiful
and expressive feature.
It is the earth's eye,
looking into which
the beholder measures
the depth of his own nature.*

Henry David Thoreau

110

Young whitebark pine overlook
Wizard Island on a crisp October morning.
Crater Lake, Oregon

Mt. Ranier, Washington

Mt. Rainier in northwestern Washington rises to a summit of 14,411 feet. It is the highest peak in the Cascade Range and the fifth highest in the United States south of Alaska. In the lower forty-eight states, only Telescope Peak in California rises higher above its surrounding landscape.

Picoides albolariatus

— White-headed Woodpecker —

The majestic Mount Rainier

112

Twenty-six glaciers are currently active on Mt. Rainier. Glaciers appear to be lifeless; but they actually support several forms of life, including mountain goats, birds who feed on insects stranded on the glaciers by strong winds, and a species of algae that sometimes grows so profusely that it turns the glaciers pink.

vaccinium membranaceum

— Thinleaf Huckleberry —

Found 5,500 feet up the mountain, Paradise Point averages almost fifty feet of snow per year.

Narada Falls on Mount Rainier

anemone
oregana

—Blue
Anemone—

The excessive moisture from the
snow and the glaciers creates lush
forests and wildflower meadows at
the mountain's base. Pacific trillium,
three-leaf anemone, calypso, and
other colorful blossoms are plentiful

113

Procyon lotor
—Raccoon—

More than fifty species of mammals,
including mountain goats that climb
to heights of 9,000 feet and 130 different species of birds, inhabit Mt.
Rainier's slopes and valleys.

In caves beneath the summit, steam
from the volcano's internal fires
heats the rock to temperatures as
high as 170° F; a few feet away from
the rocks, the air can be as cold as
0° F. Outside the caves, readings
sink to -80° F. This difference is one
of the greatest temperature ranges
ever recorded in a single place.

Potentilla
fruticosa

—Shrubby Cinquefoil—

In 1870, P. B. Van Trump and Haz-
ard Stevens were the first to reach
Mt. Rainier's summit.

*Nature never wears a mean
appearance. Neither does
the wisest man extort her secret
and lose his curiosity by finding
out all her perfection.
Nature never became a
toy to a wise spirit.
The flowers, the animals,
the mountains, reflected
the wisdom of his best hour,
as much as they had delighted
the simplicity of his childhood.*

Ralph Waldo Emerson

114

A cascade of wildflowers brighten a
July morning in Paradise Park.
Mt. Rainier, Washington

GLACIER NATIONAL PARK, MONTANA

In the Rocky Mountains of Montana, more than fifty glaciers are still actively shaping the landscape. The largest of these glaciers is Sperry Glacier, which is expanding at a rate of thirty feet per year. Grinnel Glacier covers almost 300 acres and is nearly as large as Sperry.

Lake McDonald

Woman climbing Grinnel Glacier, 1924

Orange-gilled Waxy Cap

Hygrophorus marginatus

Glaciers have been active in northwestern Montana for thousands of years. Their legacy lies in the rugged, sculpted peaks of the mountains, the deep, broad valley, and the more than 200 lakes and 936 miles of rivers and streams that flow through the area.

116

Picea engelmannii —Engelmann Spruce—

Heavens Peak rises in Glacier National Park

Beargrass is a common flower in Montana's mountain valleys. Actually, it is not grass, but a lily. Captain William Clark, of the legendary Lewis and Clark expedition, gave beargrass its name after discovering a group of bears standing in a field of the lovely white flowers.

Xerophyllum tenax
—Beargrass—

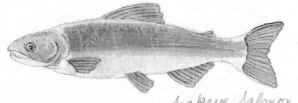

Oncorhynchus nerka

—Sockeye Salmon—

Each autumn, spawning salmon return to Flathead Lake. Following close behind are the grizzlies and the bald eagles, who come for the easy fishing.

Haliaeetus leucocephalus
—Bald Eagle—

117

Fewer than two dozen bald eagles regularly make their home in the area; salmon-spawning season, however, draws more than 400 bald eagles to Flathead Lake.

Many Glacier Hotel

Lobby of Many Glacier Hotel

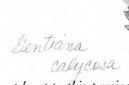

Gentiana calycosa

Give a month at least to this precious reserve. The time will not be taken from the sum of your life. Instead, it will indefinitely lengthen it and make you truly immortal.

John Muir

—Explorer's Gentian—

118

*Flowers bloom and flowers fade,
the seasons come
and the seasons go,
men are born and men die,
the world mourns for its
saints and heroes,
its poets and saviours,
but Nature remains and is as
young and spontaneous
and inexhaustible as ever.*

John Burroughs

Beauty and tranquility reign on Wild Goose
Island in St. Mary Lake.
Glacier National Park, Montana

Old Faithful, Wyoming

Old Faithful is the best known of 300 geysers within Yellowstone National Park in northwestern Wyoming. One quarter of the world's geysers are located within one square mile of Yellowstone's Upper Geyser Basin.

allium acuminatum

- Hooker's Onion -

120

Old Faithful Geyser

Punchbowl Springs, another thermal feature in Yellowstone

More than 10,000 thermal features exist in this part of Wyoming. The amazing quantity is due to the thickness of the earth's crust, the material separating the surface land from the earth's molten core. Elsewhere, the average thickness of the crust is fifteen to thirty miles; inside Yellowstone, the crust is as thin as two miles.

Riverside Geyser erupts

Hot water and steam are everywhere at Yellowstone

121

On average, Old Faithful erupts every seventy-seven minutes and sends over 8,000 gallons of water shooting up to 200 feet into the air.

Felis rufus

— Bobcat —

All of Old Faithful's eruptions are timed, measured, and recorded by park rangers. After each one, a sign predicting the next eruption is posted. These predictions are generally correct within ten minutes.

Lagopus mutus

— Rock Ptarmigan —

Old Faithful is not the largest of Yellowstone's geysers; Steamboat Geyser sends its stream of water 400 feet skyward.

mustela vison

— Mink —

We had within a distance of fifty miles seen what we believed to be the greatest wonder of the continent. . . . Judge, then, of our astonishment on entering this basin, to see at no great distance before us an immense body of sparkling water, projected suddenly and with terrific force into the air to the height of over one hundred feet. We had found a real geyser.

Nathaniel Langford

122

Old Faithful erupts on schedule to the
delight of watching visitors.
Old Faithful, Wyoming

GRAND CANYON OF YELLOWSTONE, WYOMING

The Grand Canyon of Yellowstone is a spectacular 1500-foot-deep canyon on the Yellowstone River.

Tamiasciurus hudsonicus

-Red Squirrel-

124

The awesome cascade of water into the Grand Canyon of Yellowstone

Officer's Row in Yellowstone National Park, 1898

alces alces

-Moose-

The river enters the canyon by way of a spectacular two-part waterfall. Upper Falls is a 109-foot drop; Lower Falls is nearly three times this height, twice as high as Niagara Falls.

The Yellowstone area was discovered in 1806 by John Colter, a member of the Lewis and Clark expedition who broke from the group to hunt and trap on his own.

vicia americana

— American Vetch —

Osprey and white pelicans hunt for fish from the Yellowstone River. The osprey uses its five-foot wingspan to float above the water in search of prey. White pelicans hunt in groups, slapping the water with their wings to herd the fish into shallow pools.

Pandion haliaetus

— Osprey —

Car along Madison River, 1917

Moose, bison, and bear are among the largest mammals that frequent the banks of the Yellowstone river and the nearby pine forests.

125

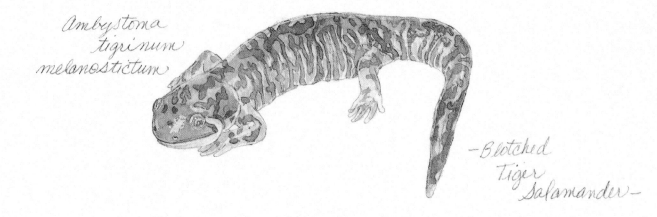

Ambystoma tigrinum melanostictum

— Blotched Tiger Salamander —

It is for itself and the moment it is enjoyed. . . . There is nothing else that has this quality so purely. . . . It therefore results that the enjoyment of scenery employs the mind without fatigue and yet exercises it; tranquilizes it, yet enlivens it; and thus, through the influence of the mind over the body, gives the effect of refreshing rest and reinvigoration to the whole system.

Frederick Law Olmstead

126

From Artist Point, the rushing
waters of the Lower Falls cascade
through a valley of the canyon.
Grand Canyon of Yellowstone, Wyoming

GRAND TETONS, WYOMING

The Grand Tetons are located in northwestern Wyoming and are part of the Rocky Mountain range. The tallest of these peaks is Grand Teton, which stands 13,770 feet above sea level.

Aquilegia coerulea

- Blue Columbine -

128

The jagged peaks of the Grand Tetons rise behind a peaceful mountain meadow

The Grand Tetons rise dramatically from the broad, flat valley of Jackson Hole. With no intervening foothills, the craggy peaks of the Tetons stand 7,000 feet above the valley floor.

- Beaver -
Castor canadensis

The first explorer to see the Grand Tetons was John Colter, a member of the Lewis and Clark expedition. His reports of abundant beaver brought a stream of trappers to the area.

Cygnus buccinator

— Trumpeter Swan —

A view of the Tetons from Signal Mountain

One of the distinctive birds of the area is the trumpeter swan, which was almost extinct before it found refuge in the shadow of these great mountains.

The Snake River winds its way across the valley floor

Ovis canadensis

— Bighorn Sheep —

After nearly disappearing from the area, elk have returned in great numbers to the Grand Tetons. Herds today are estimated at 7,500 to 10,000. In addition to the elk, bison, moose, and bighorn sheep thrive in the area.

The Snake River, which flows southward through the Grand Tetons, is home to a wide variety of birds. Bald eagles and great blue herons feed on the abundance of fish in the river, and Canada geese and trumpeter swans nest and rear their young on the riverbanks.

— Great Blue Heron —

Ardea herodias

*Mountains are, to the rest of the
body of the earth, what violent
muscular action is to the body of
man. The muscles and tendons of
its anatomy are, in the mountain,
brought out with fierce, compulsive
energy, full of expression, passion,
and strength. . . . The best image
that the world can give of Paradise
is in the slope . . . of a great alp,
with its purple rocks and eternal
snows above.*

John Ruskin

130

Jagged mountain peaks rise dramatically behind
the Snake River on a peaceful September morning.
Grand Tetons, Wyoming

BADLANDS, SOUTH DAKOTA

The Badlands are 6,000 square miles of treeless plains cut and eroded into jagged hills in South Dakota and Nebraska. The name comes from the Sioux term *mako sica*, which means "bad land to travel over."

Arctomecon merriami

-Great Desert Poppy-

132

The mysterious landscape of the Badlands

Scaphiopus bombifrons

- Plains Spadefoot -

The stripes of color on the Badlands' hills are evidence that this land was once a level plain. Gradually, the streams flowing from the Black Hills have cut into the plain and created hills and gullies that reveal the colorful layers of mudstone and siltstone.

Temperatures in the Badlands range from 115° F in the summer to 30° F in the winter. Average annual rainfall is only sixteen inches.

Antilocapra americana

-Pronghorn-

The fastest mammal on the North American continent, the pronghorn deer, thrives in the Badlands. The pronghorn reaches speeds as high as sixty miles per hour and feeds on the fifty different species of grass that grow in the area, including buffalo grass, western wheat grass, and needle-and-thread.

Near Cedar Pass in the South Dakota Badlands

133

Ancient fossils found in the Badlands reveal that the area was once covered by a shallow inland sea and inhabited by such creatures as a twelve-foot-long ancestor of the turtle.

In 1963, the National Park Service introduced a herd of fifty-three bison to the hills of the Badlands. Today, the herd has grown to 300.

-Desert Mariposa Lily-

Calochortus kennedyi

134

*Viewed at a distance, these lands
exhibit the appearance of extensive
villages and ancient castles, but
under forms so extraordinary, and
so capricious a style of
architecture, that we might consider
them as appertaining to some new
world, or ages far remote.*

Fray Pierre-Jean DeSmet

The August sun rises over the Pinnacles.
Badlands, South Dakota

THE SPLENDOR OF ALASKA AND HAWAII

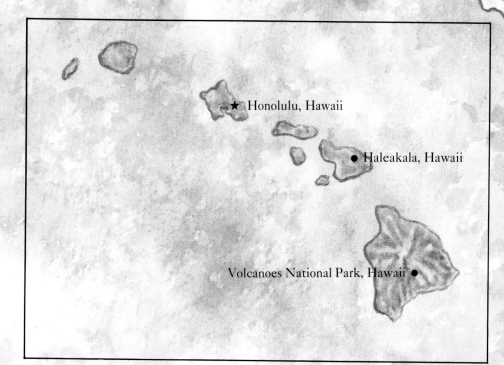

★ Honolulu, Hawaii

● Haleakala, Hawaii

Volcanoes National Park, Hawaii ●

Alaska, with its mountains carved by ice, and Hawaii, with its mountains raised by fire, are opposite extremes; yet both are majestic and mysterious, and both inspire our imaginations.

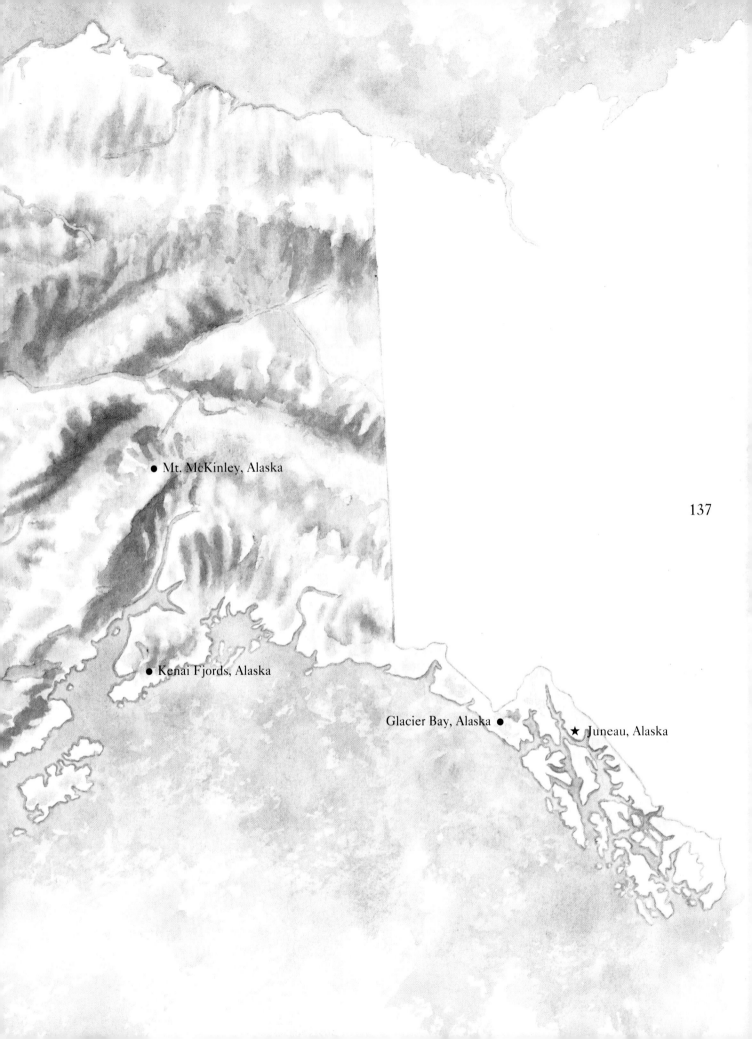

● Mt. McKinley, Alaska

137

● Kenai Fjords, Alaska

Glacier Bay, Alaska ●   ★ Juneau, Alaska

KENAI FJORDS, ALASKA

Enhydris lutris

- Sea Otter -

Kenai Fjords is found on the southern coast of Alaska, directly south of Anchorage on the Gulf of Alaska.

The sparkling blue waters of Kenai Fjords National Park

138

Fratercula cirrhata

- Tufted Puffin -

Kenai Fjords received its name from the series of steep-walled ocean inlets along the southeastern Alaskan coast. Behind the great fjords rises the Kenai Mountain range, which is covered almost entirely by the Harding Icefield, the 700-foot remainder of a glacier that once covered most of southern Alaska.

The fjords were formed as the glacier retreated from the coast and left deep gorges that were filled by the waters of the gulf.

When the climate does not allow snow to melt from one winter to the next, glaciers form. The effects of gravity combine with the continual increase or decrease of the glacier's own weight to move the large ice mass.

A humpback whale dives into the frigid Alaskan waters

Orcinus orca

-Killer Whale-

139

Kenai is home to an enormous sampling of wildlife. Bald eagles, mountain goats, wolverines, moose, bears, sea lions, harbor seals, porpoises, otters, horned puffins, sea otters, gray, humpback, and killer whales, and thousands of seabirds can be found in the waters and on the icy shorelines.

Arctostaphylos uva-ursi

-Kinnikinnick-

A mountain goat stands high atop the ice field

*The West of which I speak
is but another name for the wild,
and what I have been preparing
to say is that the Wilderness
is the preservation of the world.
Every tree sends forth its fibre
in search of the Wild.
The cities import it at any price. . . .
From the forest and Wilderness
come the tonics and the barks
which brace mankind.*

Henry David Thoreau

140

Scattered icebergs lie on the beach before
a glacier in Aialik Bay on a July afternoon.
Kenai Fjords, Alaska

Mt. McKinley, Alaska

Mt. McKinley towers above the other massive peaks of the Alaska Range. The mountain has two peaks: South Peak at 20,320 feet and North Peak at 19,470 feet. Mt. McKinley is the highest point on the North American continent; in terms of rise from the land at its base, it is the highest mountain in the world, rising 18,000 feet from base to summit.

142

Lepus americanus
— Snowshoe Hare —

The breathtaking Mt. McKinley

1913 expedition on Mt. McKinley

The timberline on Mt. McKinley lies at 2,700 feet; above this point are only ice and snow. In comparison, the timberline in the Colorado Rockies is at 11,000 to 12,000 feet.

Silpha lapponica
— Carrion Beetle —

The landscape below Mount McKinley is under snow cover from October to May.

ursus arctos

— Grizzly Bear —

Thirty-seven different mammals, including caribou, Dall sheep, and grizzly bears, make their home on or near Mt. McKinley.

Although only a thin layer of topsoil thaws each spring to support plant life, 430 species of flowering plants grace the slopes of Denali National Park during the brief warm spring and summer months.

Rhododendron albiflorum

— Cascade Azalea —

143

A 1932 attempt on Mt. McKinley

Despite the mountain's massive size, summer visitors often leave without a glimpse of Mt. McKinley, which is covered by clouds for three quarters of the summer season.

In 1903, the first group to attempt to climb Mt. McKinley made it to 8,000 feet. The successful 1913 expedition was led by Hudson Stuck, archdeacon of the Episcopal Church in Alaska. Harry Karstens, who would become first superintendent of Mt. McKinley National Park, also completed the climb.

More than 3,500 people have reached the mountain's summit since the first successful expedition in 1913.

The first attempt to conquer McKinley, 1903

*If the moon looks larger here than
in Europe, probably the sun
looks larger also.
If the heavens of America appear
infinitely higher, and the stars
brighter, I trust that these facts are
symbolical of the height to which the
philosophy and poetry and
religion of her inhabitants
may one day soar. . . .
For I believe that climate does thus
react on man—and as there is
something in the mountain-air that
feeds the spirit and inspires.*

Henry David Thoreau

144

Cotton grass surrounds Kettle Pond on an August
afternoon in Denali National Park.
Mt. McKinley Alaska

GLACIER BAY, ALASKA

Ambystoma macrodactylum

—Long-toed Salamander—

Glacier Bay is a glacier-carved inlet located in southeastern Alaska.

The vast expanse of an Alaskan glacier

146

When British explorer George Vancouver charted Alaska's coastline in the late 1700s, Glacier Bay was still filled with a massive wall of glacial ice. When John Muir visited in 1879, the glacier had retreated and left the beautiful bay. Today, the glacier has retreated a total of sixty-five miles.

Plectrophenax hyperboreus

—McKay's Bunting—

Such purity, such color, such delicate beauty! I was tempted to stay there and feast my soul, and softly freeze, until I would become part of the glacier.

John Muir

A lush rain forest thick with spruce and hemlock stands at the mouth of the bay. Nearer the glacier, the plant life changes and adapts, shrinking and finally disappearing at the foot of the great retreating ice field.

Picea mariana

—Black Spruce—

Killer whales are common in Glacier Bay. Each of these magnificent creatures measures about thirty feet in length. They feed on the bay's rich supply of fish. In addition, the humpback whale migrates 3,000 miles from its winter home off Hawaii to summer in Alaskan waters.

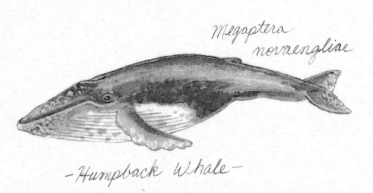

Megaptera novaengliae

—Humpback Whale—

147

The magnificent humpback whale

Here one learns that the world, though made, is yet being made; that this is still the morning of creation; that mountains long conceived are being born, channels traced for coming rivers, basins hollowed for lakes; that moraine soil is being ground and spread for coming plants . . . on predestined landscapes, to be followed by still others in endless rhythm and beauty.

John Muir

148

Stranded icebergs fill the water
as the sun sets over the bay.
Glacier Bay, Alaska

HALEAKALA, HAWAII

Haleakala Volcano is located on the island of Maui in the state of Hawaii. Its name means "house of the sun" in Hawaiian.

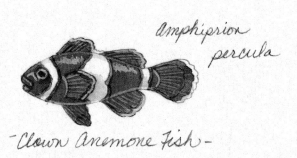

amphiprion percula

- Clown Anemone Fish -

Haleakala Crater from Haleakala Observatory

Hikers at Pele's Paint Pot

150

Red Hill, the summit of Haleakala, is 10,023 feet above sea level. It is the highest point on the island of Maui.

Puu O Maui from Ka Moa O Pele

Anthurium andraenum - Anthurium

Gradual erosion during a long period of torrential rains, not volcanic eruptions, created the crater at the mountain's peak. The crater sinks 2000 feet into the volcano's core.

Kahehameha Butterfly

Vanessa tameamea

Kamoalii Cinder Cone

Haleakala's massive bulk creates two distinct climates. On the eastern side is a lush, tropical paradise, averaging 250 inches of rainfall each year. The western side, however, receives virtually no moisture and is a stark desert.

Haleakala's last eruption occurred around the year 1790. The exact date is unknown, but the estimate is considered accurate because explorers to the area in 1786 and 1793 brought back maps that showed dramatic changes in Maui's topography, changes that could occur only through the violence of a major eruption.

Sula leucogaster

Brown Booby

151

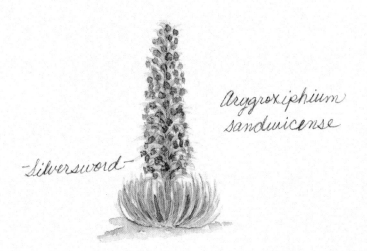

Argyroxiphium sandwicense

Silversword

Silversword in bloom

Silversword, a plant known in Hawaiian as *ahinahina*, which translates as the word gray twice, is unique to Haleakala. Growing unexpectedly in the desert of the western slopes, silversword has dagger-shaped, silvery leaves that rise to form a rosette. At maturity, it flowers briefly and dies, but not before spreading its seed for a new generation.

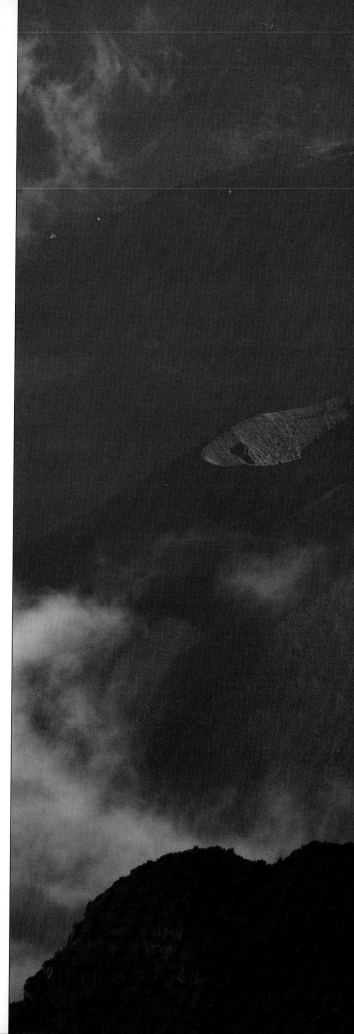

*No alien land in all the world
has any deep strong charm for me
but Hawaii, no other land could so
longingly and beseechingly haunt
me, sleeping and waking, through
half a lifetime, as that one has
done. Other things leave me, but it
abides; other things change, but it
remains the same. For me, its
balmy airs are always
blowing . . . . In my nostrils still
lives the breath of flowers that
perished twenty years ago.*

Mark Twain

152

An aerial view reveals the clouds
partially hiding the volcano's crater.
Haleakala, Hawaii

Volcanoes National Park, Hawaii

Five volcanoes—Mauna Kea, Mauna Loa, Kohala, Hualalai, and Kilauea—make up the Big Island of Hawaii. Mauna Loa and Kiluea are among the most active volcanoes on earth.

Vestiaria coccinea

-Jiwi-

154

The volcanoes do not have the pointed peaks we might expect. Their tops are cone-shaped calderas, giant craters resulting from collapsed peaks. Kilauea's caldera is two miles wide and two miles long and surrounded by jagged cliffs 400 feet high.

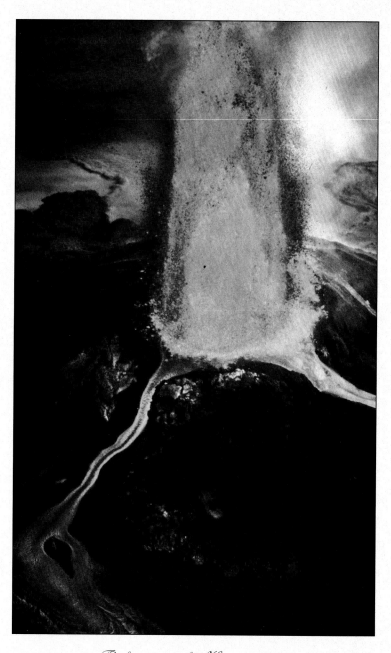

The fiery spray of a Hawaiian eruption

Chelonia mydas

-Green Turtle-

The summit of Mauna Loa in Hawaii is 13,667 feet above sea level. While this is an impressive height, if the volcano were to be measured from its base on the ocean floor, Mauna Loa would be one of the tallest mountain masses in the entire world.

At their beginning, the Hawaiian Islands were desolate mounds of solidified lava isolated in the middle of the Pacific Ocean. The wind, the waves, and an occasional far-ranging bird brought life to the islands. Eventually, Hawaii developed flora and fauna of its own, including 1,500 distinct seed plants.

Passiflora vitifolia

— Red Passion Vine —

155

Puii O O Cone Kilaula East Rift Zone with Kupaianaha lava shield and lake in foreground

Monachus shauinslandi

— Hawaiian Monk Seal —

Mammals had a more difficult time reaching the Hawaiian islands than plant life did. Only the bat and the seal made their home on Hawaii independent of man; all other species have been imported by human hands.

O God! when Thou dost scare the world with tempests, set on fire the heavens with falling thunderbolts, or fill, with all the waters of the firmament, the swift dark whirl-wind . . . when, at Thy call, uprises the great deep and throws himself upon the continent, and overwhelms its cities—who forgets not, at the sight of these tremendous tokens of Thy power, his pride and lays his strifes and follies by?

William Cullen Bryant

156

Steam clouds rise as Kupaianaha's lava flow enters the seas on a February afternoon on the Puna Coast. Volcanoes National Park, Hawaii

GEOGRAPHICAL INDEX

158

SITE INDEX

159

AUTHOR INDEX

A
B
C
D
E
F
G
H
I
J

1
2
3
4
5
6
7
8
9
0